Paper Craft Fun for Holidays

Paper Crafts for Day of the Dead

Randel McGee

Enslow Elementary
an imprint of
Enslow Publishers, Inc.
40 Industrial Road
Box 398
Berkeley Heights, NJ 07922
USA
http://www.enslow.com

Para mi esposa querida, Marsha! RM

Note to Parents and Teachers: The author uses Crayola® Model Magic® in these crafts. Other forms of air-drying modeling material may be used. Follow all package directions.

This book meets the National Standards for Arts Education standards.

Enslow Elementary, an imprint of Enslow Publishers, Inc.

Library of Congress Cataloging-in-Publication Data

McGee, Randel.
Paper crafts for Day of the Dead / Randel McGee.
p. cm. — (Paper craft fun for holidays)
Includes bibliographical references and index.
Summary: "Explains the significance of the Day of the Dead celebration and how to make crafts out of paper"—Provided by publisher.
ISBN-13: 978-0-7660-2951-4
ISBN-10: 0-7660-2951-4
1. Holiday decorations—Juvenile literature. 2. Paper work—Juvenile literature. 3. All Souls' Day—Juvenile literature. 4. All Souls' Day in art—Juvenile literature. I. Title.
TT900.H6M34 2008
745.594'1—dc22 2007013987

Printed in the United States of America

10 9 8 7 6 5 4 3 2 1

To Our Readers:
We have done our best to make sure all Internet Addresses in this book were active and appropriate when we went to press. However, the author and the publisher have no control over and assume no liability for the material available on those Internet sites or on other Web sites they may link to. Any comments or suggestions can be sent by e-mail to comments@enslow.com or to the address on the back cover.

Every effort has been made to locate all copyright holders of material used in this book. If any errors or omissions have occurred, corrections will be made in future editions of this book.

Illustration Credits: Crafts prepared by Randel McGee; Photography by Nicole diMella/Enslow Publishers, Inc.

Contents

Day of the Dead
Día de los Muertos

Día de los Muertos (DEE-ah day los moo-AIR-toes) is Spanish and means "Day of the Dead" in English. This may sound like the title of a scary movie, but it is really a fun and happy holiday in Mexico and many other countries throughout the Americas. It is somewhat like the United States's holidays of Halloween and Memorial Day rolled into one. The day is based on an Aztec celebration and the holidays of All Souls' Day and All Saints' Day, both holidays for honoring the dead. On November 1 and 2, it is believed that the spirits of those who have died can return to Earth and visit their living family and friends. Even though the living cannot see the spirits of their loved ones, they do everything they can to make them feel welcome.

To welcome and honor these ghostly guests, their living relatives make sure to have their pictures out where all can see them. Families will make little displays called *nichos* (KNEE-choes), or dioramas, of happy skeletons, representing the spirits of the dead, doing things they liked to do while they were alive such as playing games, working, and other activities. Skeletons, or *calacas* (kah-LAH-kahs), decorate everything. People also set a table with the

departed loved one's favorite foods and drinks and favorite tools, toys, kitchen utensils, or musical instruments. People throughout Mexico decorate their homes with many strings of lacy tissue-paper banners with designs cut in them called *papel picado* or *papel cortado* (PAH-pel pee-KAH-doh or cor-TAH-doh).

Mexican families visit the gravesites of their loved ones and place bright marigold flowers or *cempasúchil* (sem-pah-SU-chil) on their graves. Families have picnics in the cemetery. Some people buy sugar skulls called *calaveras* (kah-lah-VAIR-ahs). They eat a special bread made just for that day called *pan de los muertos* (pahn day los moo-AIR-toes) or "bread of the dead." Parents tell their children stories from the lives of their ancestors so that they can know them better. Families in some places will spend the whole night in the cemetery visiting, telling stories, and singing.

Marigolds are used to decorate altars and graves.

This holiday is celebrated a bit differently in each place. In some rural towns and villages they have parades or other gatherings. Those in the parade wear masks and costumes. Some towns celebrate with feasts and parties. Different foods are eaten during this celebration. People in some villages prepare special *tamales* (tah-MAH-lays). Tamales are made with corn dough that is wrapped around either spicy meat for a meal or fruit for a dessert. In more urban areas, the day is quietly celebrated with personal family get-togethers.

Paper Marigolds

In Mexico, the sunny-looking marigold flower is called *cempasúchil*. It is known as the "Flower of the Dead" and is used in Day of the Dead decorations and memorials. Use these flowers to decorate a room or a display of family pictures.

What you will need

- yellow or orange and green construction paper
- pencil
- ruler
- scissors
- white glue
- clear tape

Make your own marigold out of paper.

What to do

1. Draw different-sized circles on yellow or orange construction paper. See page 39 for the pattern. Cut out all the circles.

2. Cut many lines from the outside edge of each circle toward the center. Do not cut all the way to the center, just about halfway.

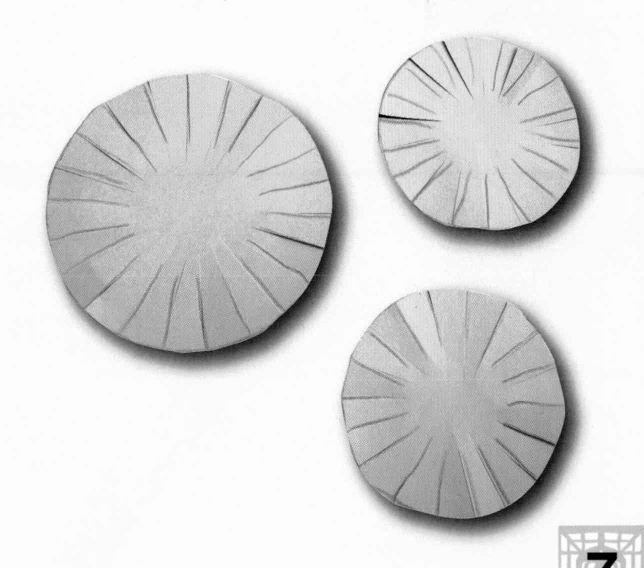

3. Each circle should now have many loose, narrow flaps. With your fingers, gently curl each flap toward the center.

4. Glue the circles together in the center so that they are layered from the smallest to the biggest circle.

5. Take a long strip of green paper 2 inches wide and roll it lengthwise so that it makes a long tube like a drinking straw. Tape the loose edge.

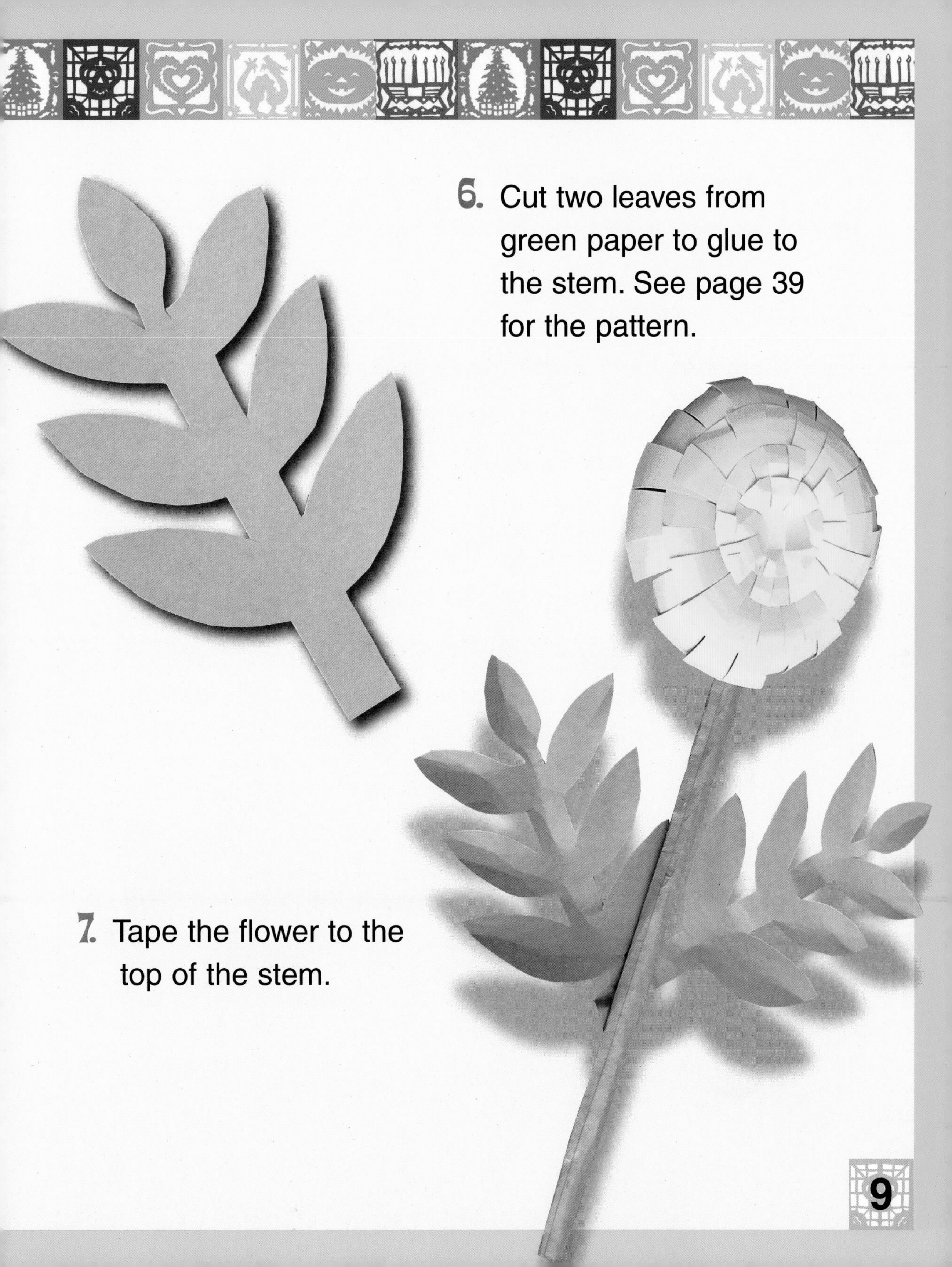

6. Cut two leaves from green paper to glue to the stem. See page 39 for the pattern.

7. Tape the flower to the top of the stem.

Skeleton Candy Basket

In Mexico, skeletons represent the ghosts of people who have died. On Day of the Dead, it is thought that the ghosts return to visit the places where they lived. Since these ghosts were once friends and relatives, they are not considered scary or evil; in fact, the ghosts like the same people, activities, and foods they did when they were alive. The skeletons look happy to be back. Candies, cookies, and other treats are made in the shape of skulls or skeletons. Make a skeleton-shaped candy basket to hold your Day of the Dead treats.

What you will need

- **8 ½-inch x 11-inch white card stock paper**
- **tracing paper**
- **pencil**
- **scissors**
- **markers or crayons**
- **clear tape**

What to do

A)

1. Fold the card stock in half so the short sides meet.

2. Use tracing paper to trace the pattern from page 40. Transfer it to the folded card stock. Make sure the flat edge of the pattern is lined up along the folded side of the paper (See A).

3. Cut out the skeleton. Cut out the shaded areas. Unfold.

4. Use markers or crayons to make a happy or silly face on the skeleton (See B).

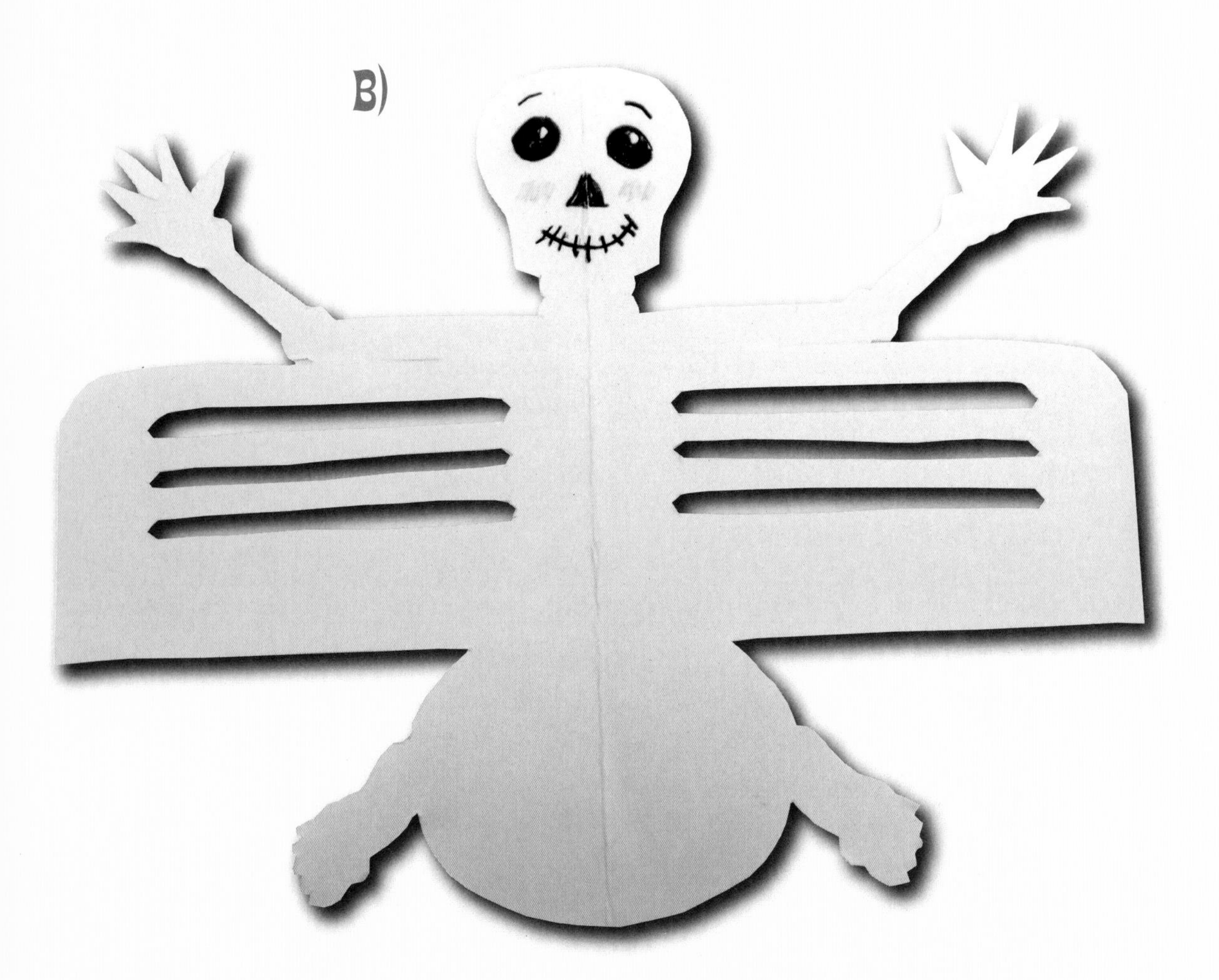

5. Pull two sides of the card stock up (the ribcage) and overlap them enough to tape them together.

6. Fold the round bottom of the basket up and use three or four short pieces of tape to fasten the bottom of the basket to the rib cage (See C).

Happy Skeleton Figures

Little skeleton figures, or *calacas*, are used as decorations all over the house. They represent deceased family and friends. They are often set in little *nichos*, three-dimensional scenes with little figures and painted backgrounds, showing them doing things they liked to do when they were alive. Here is a fun way to make your own calacas.

What you will need

- white pipe cleaners, two 12-inch and one 6-inch
- white construction paper
- scissors
- white glue
- white air-dry modeling material
- craft stick or unsharpened pencil (optional)
- markers
- yarn or string (optional)

What to do

1. Twist two 12-inch pipe cleaners together to form one thick pipe cleaner (See A).

A)

2. Bend the thick 12-inch pipe cleaner in half so that it makes an upside-down “V.” This is the start for the skeleton body. Starting at the point of the “V,” twist the top together for about one inch.

B)

3. Place the 6-inch pipe cleaner into the top of the “V” (See B). The 6-inch pipe cleaner will be the arms.

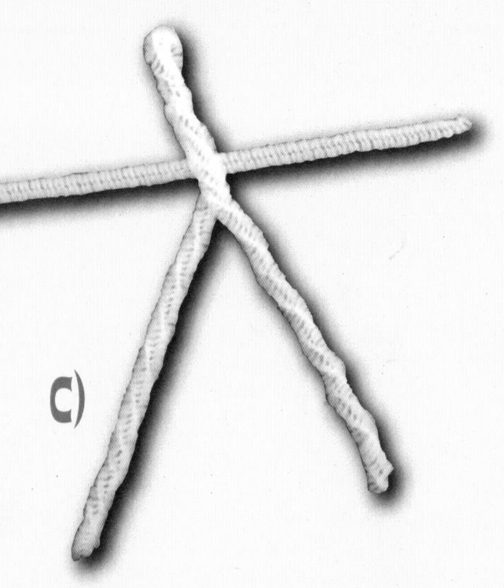

4. Twist the sides for another inch below the arms and spread them apart. These are now the legs (See C).

5. Cut some hands and a rib cage out of white construction paper and glue them in place (See D). See page 42 for the pattern.

6. Divide the white air-dry modeling material into three equal-sized pieces about the size of a cherry. Put one lump on the top for the head and the other two at the end of the legs for the feet. The feet need to be as big as the head to give the figure enough balance to stand up.

7. While the modeling material is still soft, sculpt a smiling face on the head, and toes on the feet using a pencil or craft stick. Flatten the bottom of the feet to make them stand better (See E).

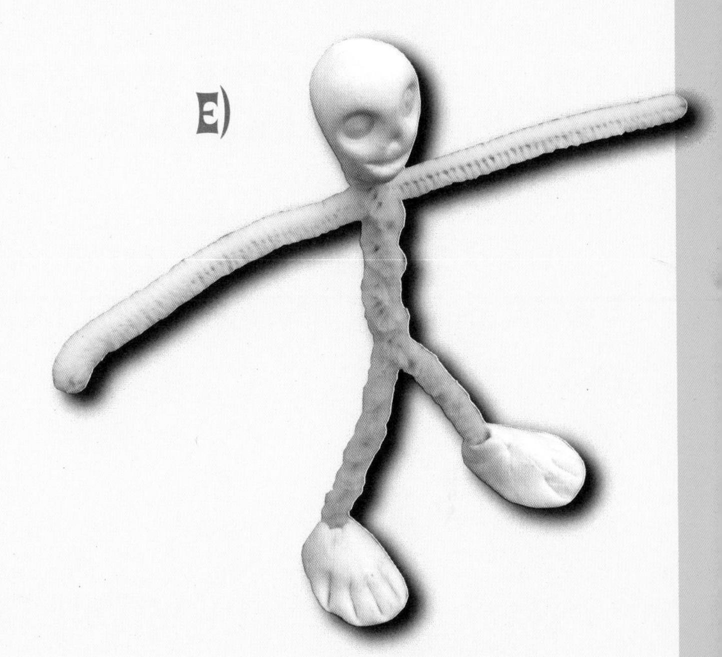

E)

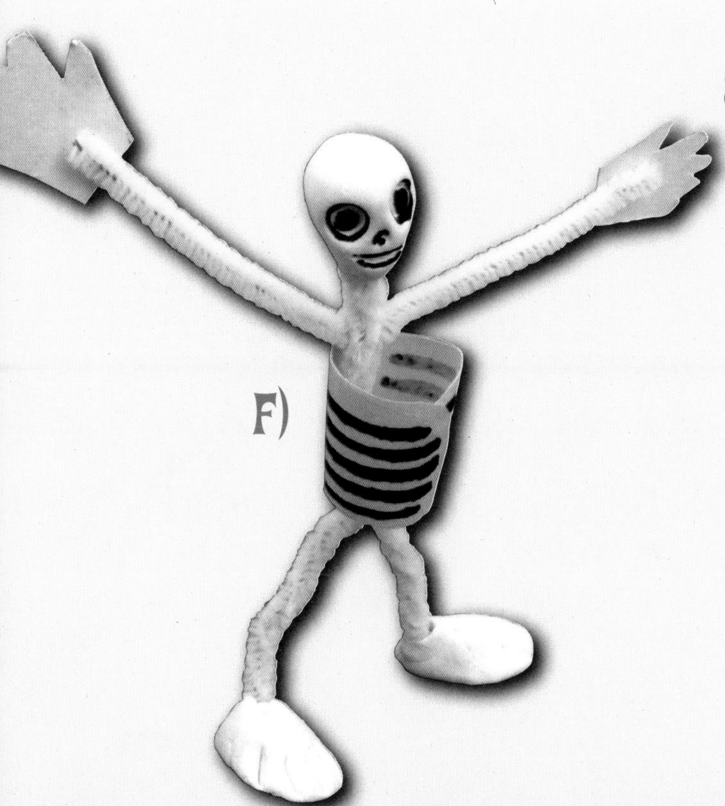

F)

8. Let the modeling material dry overnight. Once it is dry, color in the eyes and face with markers (See F). If you wish, glue on yarn or string for hair. Let dry.

Skeleton Pets

Pets are part of the family too! Here is how to make skeleton pets for your calacas to play with.

What you will need

- white pipe cleaners, 6-inch and 3-inch pieces
- white air-dry modeling material
- unsharpened pencil
- craft stick
- white construction paper
- scissors
- white glue
- markers
- yarn or string (optional)

What to do

1. Bend a 6-inch piece of pipe cleaner in half so that it makes an upside down "V" (See A). This is the start for the skeleton body. Starting at the point of the "V," twist the top together for about one inch, and then stop.

2. Place a piece of 3-inch pipe cleaner into the "V." This pipe cleaner will be the front legs.

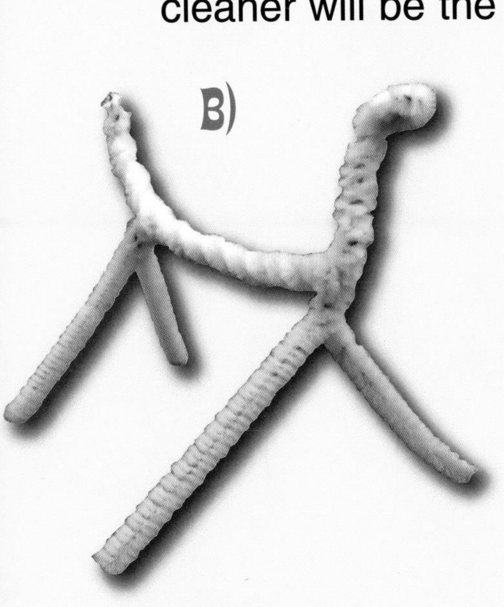

3. Twist the "V" for another inch or so. Stop and place another 3-inch pipe cleaner in the "V." This will make the back legs. Finish twisting to form the tail (See B).

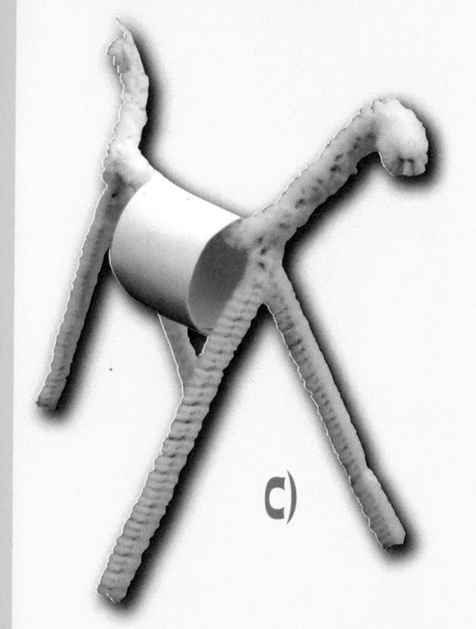

4. Divide the white air-dry modeling material into one small egg-shaped lump and four marble-sized smaller lumps. The large lump is the head and the smaller lumps are the paws. Place the large lump on the stump of the pipe cleaner body and the smaller lumps on each of the leg ends.

If you wish, add a paper rib cage (See C). See page 42 for the pattern.

5. While the modeling material is still soft, use a pencil eraser to make eyes. Use a craft stick to make the toes on the paws. Flatten the bottoms of the paws to make it stand better. While the modeling material is still soft, stick construction-paper ears into the head (See D).

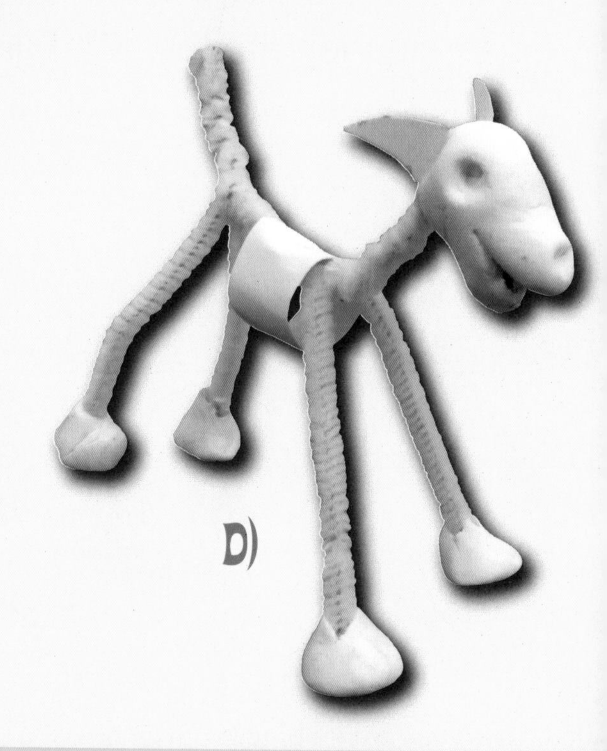

6. Let the modeling material dry. After the modeling material has dried, color in the eyes and other features with markers (See E).

7. If you wish, glue on yarn for hair, paper strips for collars, or other decorations for your pet. Let dry.

E)

Paper Clothes for the Skeletons

Calacas are often dressed in clothes similar to the ones they wore when they were living. Men wear shirts and pants, and women wear blouses and skirts or dresses. Sometimes the calacas are shown in formal clothes, since they are honored guests. Here are some patterns for clothes you can make for your calacas.

What you will need

- pencil
- tracing paper
- tissue paper or wrapping paper in any color
- scissors
- markers (optional)
- cloth scraps (optional)
- buttons (optional)
- white glue

What to do

1. Draw a shirt and pants or dress on tracing paper. See page 40 for the pattern.

2. Transfer the patterns onto a folded piece of tissue paper or wrapping paper.

3. Cut out the paper clothes.

4. Add decorations to the clothes with markers, scraps of cloth, or buttons if you wish.

5. Place the clothes on the figure and glue the loose edges of the sleeves, shirt sides, pant legs, and dresses together. Fold the loose edges in when you glue them so that the seam is on the inside of the clothes, like the ones you wear.

Skull Mask

Parades are often a part of the Day of the Dead celebration in parts of Mexico and Central America. The parades begin at night and include bands of strolling musicians and church groups carrying religious figures and banners. Some people wear skull masks that are decorated with designs in bright colors. Make your own mask.

What you will need

- 8 ½-inch x 11-inch white card stock paper
- pencil
- tracing paper
- scissors
- construction paper in any color
- markers or crayons (optional)
- craft feathers (optional)
- white glue
- masking tape
- yarn

What to do

1. Fold the white card stock paper in half lengthwise.

2. Use tracing paper to transfer the pattern from page 41 to the folded card stock. Place the flat edge of the pattern on the folded edge of the card stock.

People still wear skull masks in Mexico for Day of the Dead.

A)

3. Cut out the pattern and unfold it. Now you have a mask.

4. Cut out eyes, a nose, and a mouth (See A).

B)

5. Decorate the mask with shapes cut from the construction paper. If you wish, use markers, crayons, or feathers (See B).

6. Overlap the round flaps at the top center of the skull and glue or tape them together (See C).

7. Use masking tape to tape two lengths of yarn to both sides of the back of the mask. Make sure that the yarn is long enough to tie around your head (See D).

C)

D)

Papel Cortado Window Banners

Since ancient times in Mexico, people have used paper-thin bark to cut out designs as decorations for special events. For Day of the Dead, people decorate their windows and homes with colorful banners made of *papel cortado* or *papel picado*, or "cut paper." These are delicate, tissue-paper banners that look like lace curtains. They often contain skull and marigold designs and other shapes to fill out the banner.

What you will need

- several sheets of tissue paper in any color
- pencil
- scissors
- string or yarn
- white glue
- clear tape

What to do

1. Fold three or four sheets of tissue paper in half lengthwise.

2. Lightly draw some designs with a pencil on the tissue paper. See page 43 for the pattern.

3. Cut out the tissue-paper designs.

4. Lay several tissue-paper designs next to each other in a line.

5. Glue or tape a long length of string or yarn ¼-inch from the top edge of the tissue paper designs. Fold the top of the tissue paper over the string or yarn, and glue down. Let dry.

6. Carefully lift the tissue paper banners. Ask an adult to help you tape them to a window frame.

Aztec Animal Decorations

The Aztecs were a people that settled in the Valley of Mexico about 1200 A.D. They became a large and powerful society with huge cities of buildings and pyramids. They are the ancestors of many present-day Mexican people. Their artists decorated their buildings and pottery with animal designs. Make Aztec animal designs to decorate walls, windows, placemats, or anything you wish.

What you will need

- pencil
- tracing paper
- construction paper
- light-colored poster board
- markers or crayons
- scissors
- white glue
- clear tape
- paper cups (optional)
- placemats (optional)

What to do

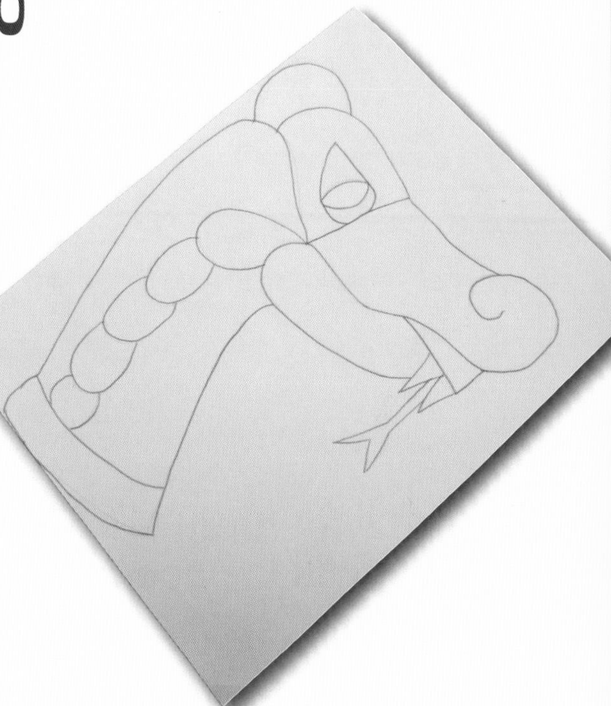

1. Trace the Aztec animal designs on page 38 on to tracing paper. Pick your favorite design.

2. Transfer the designs to light-colored construction paper or poster board.

3. Color the designs with markers or crayons. Cut them out.

4. Glue the designs to a piece of dark-colored construction paper and hang it on a wall or in a window.

5. Smaller designs may be glued on placemats and paper cups to decorate a holiday table.

The ancient Aztecs built pyramids and buildings. These ruins in Mexico show an ancient temple that was built for the Sun God.

PATTERNS

Enlarge 160% or enlarge to fit your decorations.

Use tracing paper to copy the patterns on these pages. Ask an adult to help you cut and trace the shapes.

Paper Marigolds

Enlarge 240%

Enlarge 150%

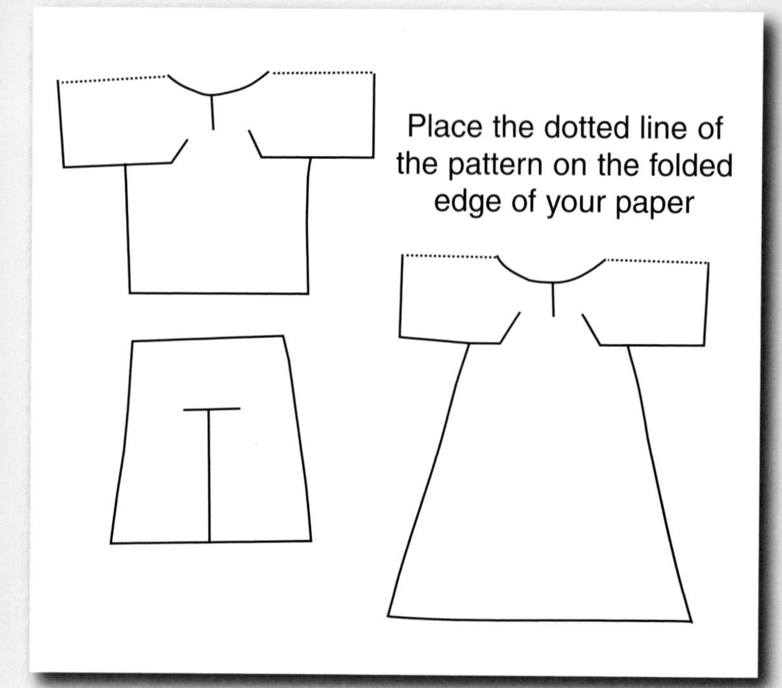

Paper Clothes for the Skeletons

Enlarge 225%

Enlarge 230%

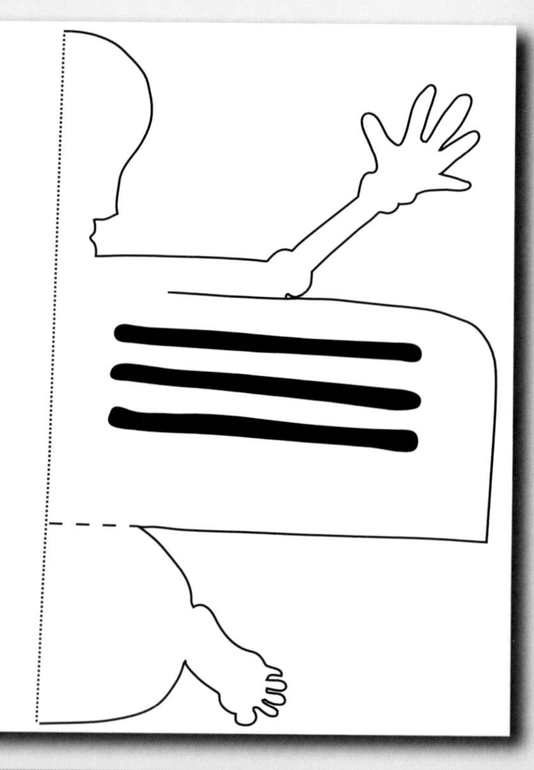

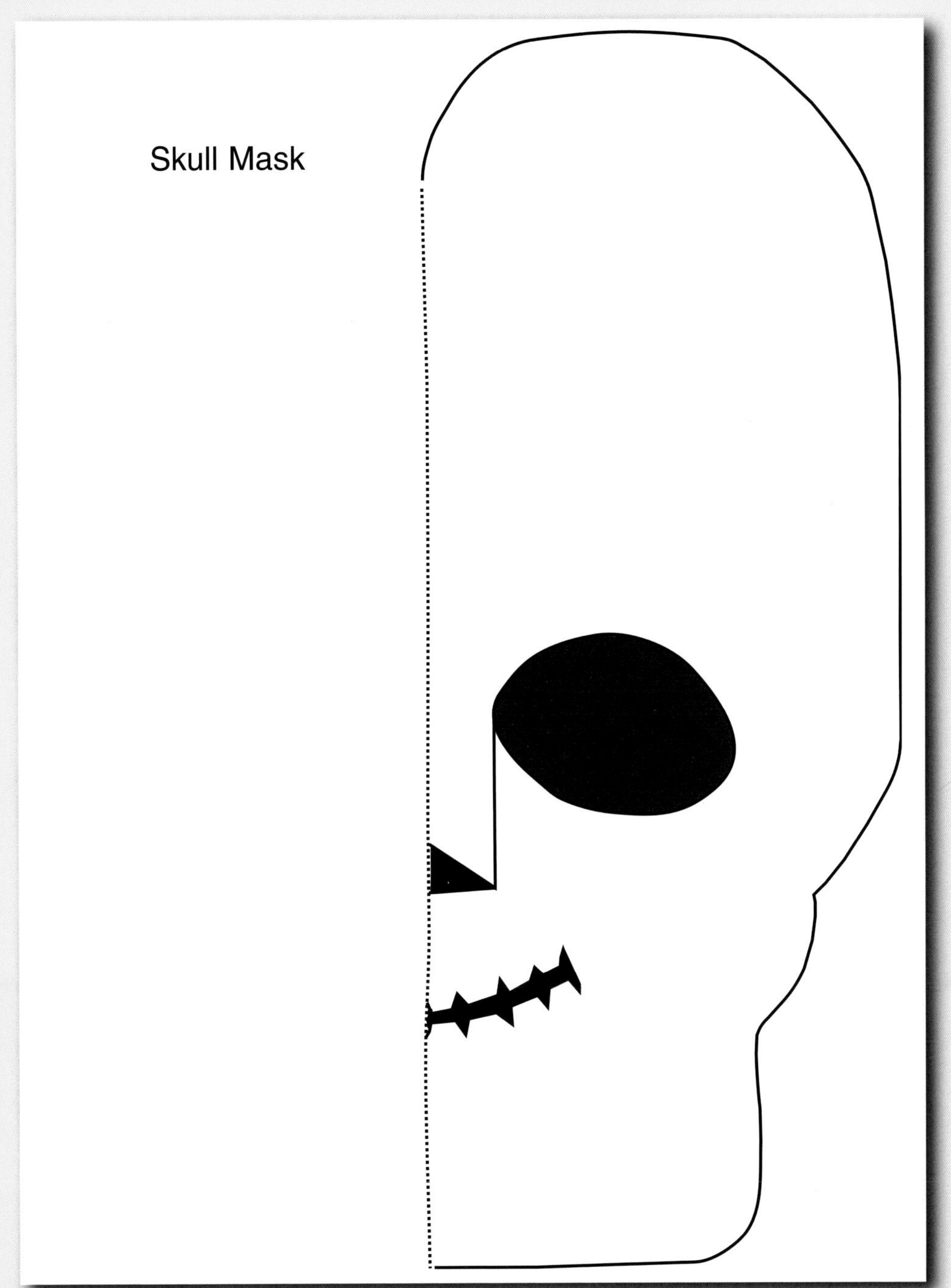

Enlarge 155%

Happy Skeleton Figures

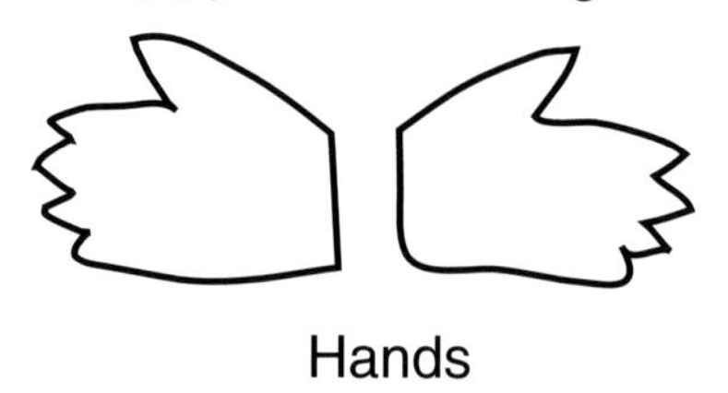

Hands

Rib Cage

Skeleton Pets

Rib Cage

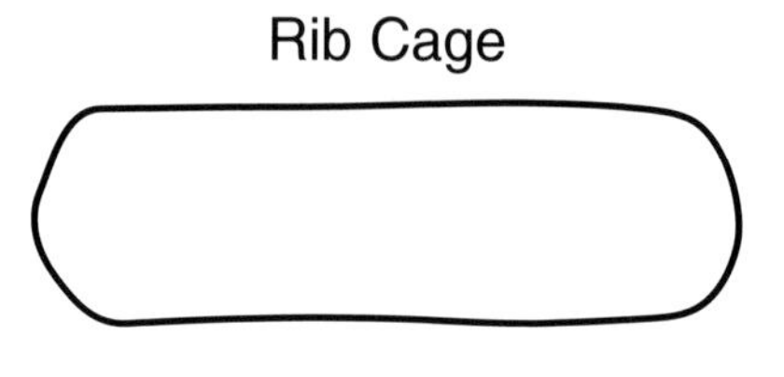

Tail

pointy dog ear

round dog ear

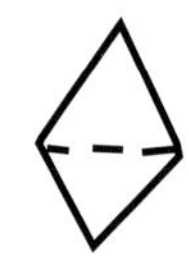

cat ear

Enlarge 145%

Papel Cortado
Window Banners

Enlarge 210%

Place the dotted line along the folded edge of the tissue paper.

Cut along all the solid lines to cut out all the dark areas.

Place the dotted line along the folded edge of the tissue paper.

Cut along all the solid lines to cut out all the dark areas.

Read About

Books

DeAngelis, Gina. *Mexico.* Mankato, Minn.: Blue Earth Books, 2003.

Doering, Amanda. *Day of the Dead: A Celebration of Life and Death.* Mankato, Minn.: Capstone Press, 2006.

Johnston, Tony. *The Ancestors Are Singing.* New York: Farrar Straus Giroux, 2003.

Kalman, Bobbie. *Mexico. The People.* New York: Crabtree, 2002.

Lowery, Linda. *Day of the Dead.* Minneapolis, Minn.: Carolrhoda Books, 2004.

Wade, Mary Dodson. *El Día de los Muertos.* New York: Children's Press, 2002.

Internet Addresses

México for Kids

<http://www.elbalero.gob.mx/index_kids.html>

What do Mexicans celebrate on the "Day of the Dead?"

<http://www.public.iastate.edu/~rjsalvad/scmfaq/muertos.html>

Visit Randel McGee's Web site at

<http://www.mcgeeproductions.com>

Index

About the Author

Randel McGee has been playing with paper and scissors for as long as he can remember. As soon as he was able to get a library card, he would go to the library and find the books that showed paper crafts, check them out, take them home, and try almost every craft in the book. He still checks out books on paper crafts at the library, but he also buys books to add to his own library and researches paper-craft sites on the Internet.

McGee says, "I begin by making copies of simple crafts or designs I see in books. Once I get the idea of how something is made, I begin to make changes to make the designs more personal. After a lot of trial and error, I find ways to do something new and different that is all my own. That's when the fun begins!"

McGee also liked singing and acting from a young age. He graduated college with a degree in children's theater and specialized in puppetry. After college, he taught himself ventriloquism and started performing at libraries and schools with a friendly dragon puppet named Groark. "Randel McGee and Groark" have toured throughout the United States and Asia, sharing their fun shows with young and old alike.

Groark is the star of two award-winning video series for elementary school students on character education: *Getting Along with Groark* and *The Six Pillars of Character.*

In the 1990s, McGee combined his love of making things with paper with his love of telling stories. He tells stories while making pictures cut from paper to illustrate the tales he tells. The famous author Hans Christian Andersen also made cut-paper pictures when he told stories. McGee portrays Andersen in storytelling performances around the world.

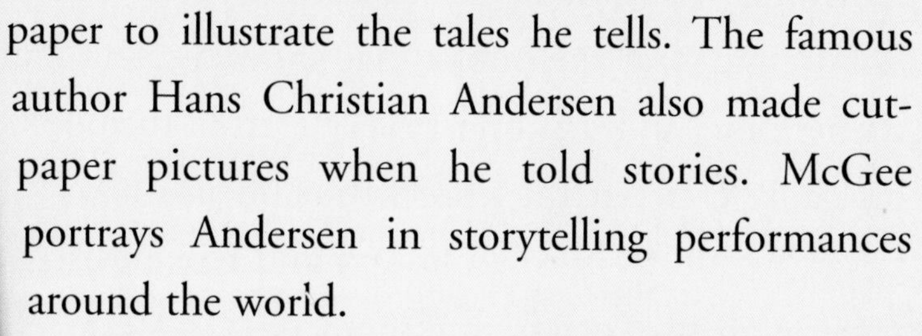

Besides performing and making things, McGee, with the help of his wife, Marsha, likes showing librarians, teachers, fellow artists, and children the fun and educational experiences they can have with paper crafts, storytelling, drama, and puppetry. Randel McGee has belonged to the Guild of American Papercutters, the National Storytelling Network, and the International Ventriloquists' Association. He has been a regional director for the Puppeteers of America, Inc., and past president of UNIMA-USA, an international puppetry organization. He has been active in working with children and scouts in his community and church for many years. He and his wife live in California. They are the parents of five grown children who are all talented artists and performers.